The Story of a Special Day
Volume 82

March

22

81st day of the year
(82nd in leap years)
284 days remaining
until the end of the year.

by Michael Dobson

Timespinner Press

For more information about the series, about me, or about your special day, please email us at editor@timespinnerpress.com.

Look for other volumes in *The Story of a Special Day*, coming often.

Table of Contents

Cover: Lasers in use at the Naval Surface Weapons Center, for the Event of the Day for March 22.

Back Cover: The month of March, from the French Gothic illuminated manuscript *Les Très Riches Heures du duc de Berry.*

March 22 Quotations

"Beauty has wings, and too hastily flies/And love, unrewarded, soon sickens and dies."

— *author Edward Moore, born March 22, 1712*

"A greater absurdity cannot be thought of than a morose, hard-hearted, covetous, proud, malicious Christian."

— *theologian Jonathan Edwards, died March 22, 1758*

"One ought, every day at least, to hear a little song, read a good poem, see a fine picture, and, if it were possible, to speak a few reasonable words."

— *philosopher Johann Wolfgang von Goethe, died March 22, 1832*

"There is no likelihood man can ever tap the power of the atom. The glib supposition of utilizing atomic energy when our coal has run out is a completely unscientific Utopian dream, a childish bug-a-boo."

— *Nobel-winning physicist Robert Millikan, born March 22, 1868*

"He never wants anything but what's right and fair; only when you come to settle what's right and fair, it's everything that he wants and nothing that you want. And that's his idea of a compromise."

— *author Thomas Hughes, born March 22, 1896*

"Stay out of the spotlight. It fades your suit."

— *Hollywood agent Lew Wasserman, born March 22, 1913*

"Never get a mime talking. He won't stop."

— *mime Marcel Marceau, born March 22, 1923*

Event of the Day

The Laser Gets a Patent

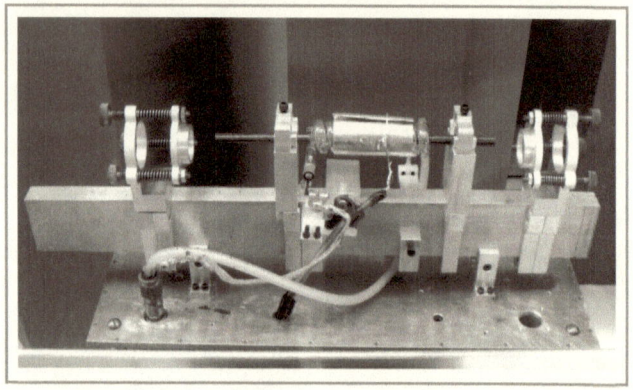

An early laser

On March 22, 1960, U.S. Patent 2,929,922 was issued to Charles Townes and his brother-in-law Arthur Schawlow, both of Bell Laboratories, for the laser. It was a key moment in both the development of laser technology, and the beginning of a 30-year patent fight over who owned and who got credit for an invention that undergirds so much modern technology: CDs and DVDs, medical applications, fiber optics, bar code scanners, and much more.

The word "laser" is an acronym: light amplification by stimulated emission of radiation. When an atom absorbs enough energy, it moves from a "ground-state" energy level to an "excited" level. To return to the ground state, the atom releases the extra energy as a particle of light, known as a *photon*. This happens in many ways: when a piece of metal glows red from being heated, it is releasing energy as photons.

In a laser, it's done more systematically. Energy is pumped into a lasing medium (early laser used rubies) and reflected through mirrors to make the resultant light *monochromatic* (all photons have the same wavelength), *coherent* (all photons move in step with one another), and *directional* (focused in an extremely tight beam). Lasers today can use a wide range of lasing materials and the resultant laser light has different properties.

The discovery that energy can be emitted or absorbed in discrete packages, known as quanta, comes from physicist Max Planck, who first published his studies in 1900.

Five years later, Albert Einstein expanded Planck's work by publishing an important paper on the photoelectric effect, showing that light also consisted of quantum particles, or photons. (It was for the photoelectric effect, not for relativity, that Einstein received his Nobel Prize.) By 1917, Einstein had developed the idea of "stimulated emission," the *"s e"* in laser.

It wasn't until 1954, however, that scientists were actually able to turn Einstein's work into a practical device. Charles Townes, Herbert Zeiger, and James Gordon, all at Columbia University, demonstrated the first laser-device, originally known as a "maser." (The "m" stood for "microwave.")

The idea of an "optical maser" that emitted light rather than microwaves came from two sources: Townes, and a graduate student named Gordon Gould, who came up with the name "laser." Gould went into private industry after having his notes about laser notarized.

Townes, who now worked for Bell Labs, meanwhile continued his work, and along with Schawlow submitted a patent application in July 1958, which was approved. Meanwhile, Gould and his company, TRG, submitted their own application in April 1959, but Townes and Schawlow had applied first.

Gould and TRG appealed, using Gould's notarized notes as evidence that he was actually the inventor of the laser, regardless of the date of application. The patent battle would go on until the late 1970s, when Gould eventually won.

Meanwhile, laser development continued. By 1960, ruby laser, uranium lasers, and helium-neon lasers had been demonstrated. The following year, the first commercial lasers came to market. The first laser was used in medicine in 1961, fiber optic lasers in 1966, telecommunications lasers in 1970, bar code scanner lasers in 1972 (the first item scanned was a pack of Wrigley's chewing gum), laser discs in 1978 — and the list goes on.

In 1964, Charles Townes and associates received a Nobel Prize in Physics for their work on maser and lasers. Gould began receiving royalties from laser applications in 1988. Today, lasers are part of everyday life, one of the most useful products to spring from early theoretical work by Max Planck and Albert Einstein.

March 22 Holidays and Celebrations

Día de la Abolición de la Esclavitud (Puerto Rico)

Emancipation Day, or the Day for the Abolition of Slavery, is a public holiday in Puerto Rico each March 22, commemorating the 1873 abolition of slavery, which took place when the island of Puerto Rico was still a Spanish colony.

Easter Season

Easter is a *moveable feast*, meaning it occurs on different days each year. The earliest date is March 22. (See the ***Easter Events*** section for more.)

Christian Feast Days

March 22 is the feast day of Saint Lea, Darerca of Ireland, Epaphroditus, Paul of Narbonne, Nicholas Owen, and Basil of Ancyra. In Eastern Orthodox Christianity, it's also the commemoration of Isaac of Dalmatia, martyr Drosida of Antioch and five nuns, martyrs Callinica and Basilissa of Rome, martyr Euthymius of Mount Athos, and martyrs Sophia of Kiev and her priest Dmitry Ivanov. (These Eastern Orthodox events are observed on April 4 by "Old Calendarists" who use the Julian calendar.)

What Happened on March 22?

The abbreviation "O.S." on some dates refers to the fact that the Russian Empire did not switch from the Julian to the Gregorian calendar at the same time as the rest of Europe, and therefore some figures have two dates for their birth or death.

People whose original names are not in the Western alphabet have their native names in the appropriate script shown in parenthesis.

1621 CE – **The Pilgrims and the Wampanoag Sign a Treaty**

Plymouth Colony, the first outpost of the Pilgrims in the New World, nearly perished during their first winter until a native American named Samoset entered the colony on March 16, 1621, saying "Welcome, Englishmen!" (Samoset had known some British fishermen and trappers in Maine.)

It was then that the colonists learned that the native tribes had suffered an epidemic of smallpox, and had been dramatically weakened.

On March 22, 1621, Samoset returned with Massasoit, the leader of the Wampanoag tribe, and the colonists and the chief negotiated a treaty of peace and mutual support, which lasted for nearly forty years.

Massasoit and Governor John Carver smoke a peace pipe

1622 CE – **Jamestown Massacre**

Jamestown, Virginia, was the site of the first successful English settlement in North America, originally founded in 1607. Within a few years, however, colonists began sending raiding parties to steal food from the Powhatan tribe.

The First Anglo-Powhatan War lasted from 1610 to 1614, ending in the Peace of Pocahontas, but continuing English encroachments led to further hostilities.

The Second Anglo-Powhatan War began on March 22, 1622, with a series of surprise attacks on Jamestown that killed 347 people, a quarter of the English population. Rather than flee, the English took their revenge, pillaging and killing Powhatans and adding substantial land to their colony.

In 1623, the Powhatan sued for peace, but at the meeting, the colonists poisoned the wine they gave the Powhatan for the ceremonial toast, and killed about 200.

1765 CE – **Stamp Act Passed**

One of the triggering events of the American Revolutionary War was the passage of the Stamp Act of 1765, which placed a tax on colonists to help pay for British troops stationed in North America. It was approved by King George III on March 22, 1765, and went into effect that November.

It was the Stamp Act that led to the phrase "no taxation without representation," because the colonists had no voice in the British Parliament. Resistance to the Stamp Act resulted in the colonists building connections and alliances that would help them later in forming a united alliance against British rule.

Protests began peacefully and grew violent, and the stamp tax was never actually collected. While Parliament repealed the Stamp Act a year later, they insisted on the right to legislate for the colonies "in all cases whatsoever."

Attempts to tax and regulate would continue over the next ten years until the outbreak of the Revolutionary War in 1775.

A Stamp Act stamp

1784 CE – **The Emerald Buddha Comes Home**

The Emerald Buddha (page 14) is a statue over a foot tall made entirely of green jadeite and clothed in gold. It was, according to legend, made in 43 BCE in India, and was sent by ship to Ceylon (Sri Lanka).

The ship got lost in a storm and the Emerald Buddha ended up in Cambodia, captured by the local rulers, and hidden. In 1434, it showed up in northern Thailand, covered in stucco to conceal its worth.

A lightning strike (again, according to legend) revealed something shiny under the stucco, and the Emerald Buddha was revealed.

Its ownership and location changed several more times, until King Rama I of Thailand moved it to its current home in Wat Phra Kaew (วัดพระแก้ว), the Temple of the Emerald Buddha, on March 22, 1784, where it remains on display.

1888 CE – **First Football League**

The world's oldest professional football (soccer) league, The Football League, was established on March 22, 1888. Originally, the league had twelve teams, which grew to 92 by 1950. The largest clubs of the Football League broke away in 1992 to form the Premier League, the highest professional league in English football.

The Emerald Buddha

1943 CE – **Khatyn Massacre**

On March 22, 1943, Nazi SS units drove the inhabitants of the Belarusian town of Khatyn into a shed, covered it with straw, and set it on fire, killing 149 people, including 75 children. Two children and one badly wounded adult survived. Over 5,000 Belarusian settlements were destroyed by Nazis in this manner, killing over 2 million people.

In the late years of the Soviet Brezhnev era, there was a lot of focus on this crime, and the village has been turned into a memorial, partially to distract attention from the similarly named *Katyn* massacre of Polish officers by the Soviet secret police.

1945 CE – **Arab League Founded**

The League of Arab States (جامعة الدول العربية), commonly known as the Arab League, was formed in Cairo on March 22, 1945, and currently has 22 members.

1972 CE – **Unmarried People in the U.S. May Possess Contraception**

In *Eisenstadt v. Baird* (405 U.S. 438), issued March 22, 1972, the Supreme Court struck down a Massachusetts law prohibiting the distribution of contraception to unmarried people.

1975 CE – **Browns Ferry Nuclear Plant Fire**

A worker using a candle to search for air leaks accidentally set a cable seal on fire at the Browns Ferry Nuclear Plant near Decatur, Alabama, on March 22, 1975. The fire spread throughout reactor building. Although it was quickly controlled, the Nuclear Regulatory Commission later concluded that the fire was more likely than any other situation except Three Mile Island to have led to a serious nuclear accident.

1978 CE – **Death of Karl Wallenda**

Karl Wallenda, founder and leader of the aerial act The Flying Wallendas, was killed on March 22, 1978, while walking on a high wire between the 10-story high towers of the Condado Plaza Hotel in San Juan, Puerto Rico. He was 73.

The Flying Wallendas performing the Seven-Man Pyramid

1984 CE – **McMartin Preschool Trial Begins**

The McMartin family, who operated a California preschool facility, were accused of sexual and Satanic ritual abuse of children. The longest, most expensive criminal trial in American history resulted. No convictions were obtained; all charges were eventually dropped.

1989 CE – **Clint Malarchuk's Throat is Cut**

During an ice hockey game on March 22, 1989, between the St. Louis Blues and the Buffalo Sabres, the skate of one of the opposing players accidentally caught Sabre goaltender Clint Malarchuk on the neck, cutting his jugular vein. The team's trainer, a former Army medic, was able to staunch the bleeding until doctors arrived, but had the skate hit 1/8" higher or at the other end of the ice, he would have died. Malarchuk did return to hockey as a player, but moved into coaching.

1993 CE – **First Pentium Chips**

On March 22, 1993, the Intel Corporation released the first computer chip carrying the Pentium name, which would be the company's flagship CPU brand for well over 20 years.

1995 CE – **Longest Stay in Space**

Cosmonaut Valeri Polyakov (Валерий Поляков) established a record for the longest single spaceflight in history: 437 days, 18 hours. He lifted off on January 8, 1994, returning to Earth on March 22, 1995.

He also held at that time the record for total time in space, but that has since been broken. Polyakov's mission proved that humans were able to remain healthy both mentally and physically on long-duration spaceflights.

1997 CE – **Youngest Gold Medalist in History**

At the age of 14, Tara Lipinski was the youngest figure skater to win a U.S. championship, became the youngest person to win a World Championship, and at the 1988 Winter Olympics became the youngest individual gold medalist in Winter Olympic history.

1997 CE – **Comet Hale-Bopp Approaches Earth**

Comet Hale-Bopp was the most widely observed 20th century comets, visible to the naked eye for a 18 months. It made its closest approach to Earth on March 22, 1997, at a distance of 1.315 AU (122 million miles, or 197 million kilometers).

Comet Hale-Bopp photographed by Philipp Salzgeber

Who Was Born on March 22?

Arts and Literature

James Patterson (March 22, 1947 —)

Best-selling thriller author James Patterson is best known for his novels about fictional psychologist Alex Cross. He set a New York *Times* record for most bestselling hardcover fiction titles (76) by a single author.

Rudy Rucker (March 22, 1946 —)

Mathematician and science fiction author Rudy Rucker won Philip K. Dick Awards for the first two novels in his Ware Tetralogy.

Billy Collins (March 22, 1941 —)

Collins was Poet Laureate of the United States from 2001 to 2003.

E. D. Hirsch Jr. (March 22, 1928 —)

Cultural and literary critic Hirsch is best known for his 1987 best-selling book *Cultural Literacy: What Every American Needs to Know.*

Nicholas Monsarrat (March 22, 1910 — August 8, 1979)

Monsarrat is best known for his sea stories, most notably *The Cruel Sea*, made into a 1953 movie.

Louis L'Amour (March 22, 1908 — June 10, 1988)

Western writer Louis L'Amour was one of the most popular writers in the world during his career. He received the Congressional Gold Medal and the Presidential Medal of Freedom for his contributions to American literature, and his 1979 novel *Bendigo Shafter* won the U.S. National Book Award.

Bill Holman (March 22, 1903 — February 27, 1987)

Cartoonist Bill Holman created and drew the comic strip *Smokey Stover* from 1935 to 1973.

Greta Kempton (March 22, 1901 — December 10, 1991)

Kempton was the White House painter in the Truman administration, creating the official portraits of the President and First Lady.

Randolph Caldecott (March 22, 1846 — February 12, 1886)

British artist Randolph Caldecott is best known for his illustrated children's books.

The Caldecott Medal, awarded annually for "the most distinguished picture book for children" is named for him.

Illustration by Randolph Caldecott for "The House that Jack Built"

Virginia Oldoini, Countess of Castiglione (March 22, 1837 — November 28, 1899)

The Italian aristocrat known as La Castiglione was a mistress of Napoleon III, but is best known for arranging 700 different photographs of herself in which she recreated her life for the camera, spending much of her fortune in the process.

Photograph of La Castiglione by Pierre-Louise Pierson

Thomas Crawford (March 22, 1814 — October 10, 1857)

American sculptor Thomas Crawford is best known for his bronze statue "Statue of Freedom," which crowns the dome of the U.S. Capitol in Washington, DC.

Statue of Freedom,
Thomas Crawford

Anton Raphael Mengs (March 22, 1728 — June 29, 1779)

German painter Anton Mengs was a court painter in Saxony and Madrid, known as a transitional figure between the Baroque and neoclassicist schools of painting.

Self-portrait, Anton Raphael Mengs

Edward Moore (March 22, 1712 — March 1, 1757)

English dramatist Edward Moore is remembered for his play *The Gamester*, first produced starring David Garrick, the leading figure in 18th century English theater. *The Gamester* is the source of the phrase "rich beyond the dreams of avarice."

Anthony van Dyck (March 22, 1599 — December 9, 1641)

Flemish Baroque painter Anthony van Dyck became England's leading court painter during the reign of Charles I. He was trained by Peter Paul Rubens and heavily influenced by Titian.

Self-portrait, Anthony van Dyck

Film, Television, and Theater

Tania Raymonde (March 22, 1952 —)

TV actress Raymonde played Cynthia in *Malcolm in the Middle* and Alex on *Lost*.

Reese Witherspoon (March 22, 1976 —)

Witherspoon is known for her roles in *Election*, *Legally Blonde*, and *Sweet Home Alabama*. She won an Academy Award, a Golden Globe, and a Screen Actors Guild award for playing June Carter Cash in *Walk the Line*.

Reese Witherspoon

Kellie Shanygne Williams (March 22, 1976 —)

Williams is best known as Laura Winslow on the TV show *Family Matters*.

Anne Dudek (March 22, 1975 —)

Dudek is known for her roles on the TV series *House, Mad Men,* and *Covert Affairs.*

Will Yun Lee (March 22, 1971 —)

Will Yun Lee is best known for playing the villain in the James Bond *film Die Another Day,* and for his TV roles on *Witchblade* and the remake of *Bionic Woman.*

Matthew Modine (March 22, 1959 —)

Modine played Private Joker in *Full Metal Jacket* and received an Emmy nomination for *And the Band Played On.*

Carlton Cuse (March 22, 1959 —)

Cuse was executive producer and screenwriter for the TV series *Lost.*

Lena Olin (March 22, 1955 —)

Olin received a Golden Globe nomination for her role in *The Unbearable Lightness of Being,* and an Oscar nod for *Enemies, a Love Story.*

Mary Tamm (March 22, 1950 — July 26, 2012)

Tamm is best known as Romana from the BBC series *Doctor Who* in the story arc "The Key of Time."

Eric Roth (March 22, 1945 —)

Roth won an Academy Award for Best Adapted Screenplay for 1994's *Forrest Gump* and was nominated three additional times.

Haing S. Ngor (吳漢潤) (March 22, 1940 — February 25, 1996)

Ngor won the Academy Award for Best Supporting Actor for his role in The Killing Fields, having experienced life in Cambodia under the Khmer Rouge. He was murdered in 1996 by members of an Oriental street gang in Los Angeles.

M. Emmet Walsh (March 22, 1935 —)

Actor Walsh has appeared in over 200 film and TV productions, and is known for his work in *The Jerk*, *Blade Runner*, and *Blood Simple*. Roger Ebert wrote, "no movie featuring either Harry Dean Stanton or M. Emmet Walsh in a supporting role can be altogether bad."

Larry Martyn (March 22, 1934 — August 7, 1944)

English TV actor Larry Martyn appeared in such series *as Are You Being Served?*, *Up Pompeii!*, and *Whoops Baghdad*.

May Britt (March 22, 1933 —)

May Britt appeared in Swedish and Italian productions before moving to the U.S. to play in such films as *The Young Lions* and *Murder, Inc.* She is best known for her controversial marriage to Sammy Davis, Jr., in a time where interracial marriage was illegal in most of the United States.

William Shatner (March 22, 1931 —)

Shatner is best known as Captain James T. Kirk from the TV and film franchise *Star Trek*.

Left: Leonard Nimoy and William Shatner

Carrie Donovan (March 22, 1928 — November 12, 2001)

Fashion editor for *Vogue* and *Harper's Bazaar*, Donovan became popularly known for appearing in Old Navy commercials, wearing large eyeglasses and black clothing and declaring the merchandise to be "fabulous!"

Gilles Pelletier (March 22, 1925 —)

Pelletier is known to Canadian audiences for playing Corporate Jacques Gagnier in the police drama *R.C.M.P.*.

Bill Wendell (March 22, 1924 — April 14, 1999)

Announcer Bill Wendell worked on *The Ernie Kovacs Show, Tic Tac Dough* and other game shows, the Macy's Thanksgiving Day Parade, and *Late Night With David Letterman*. He appeared as a TV announcer in the Billy Crystal film *Mr. Saturday Night*.

Marcel Marceau (March 22, 1923 — September 22, 2007)

French actor and mime Marcel Marceau is best known for his persona, Bip the Clown.

Ross Martin (March 22, 1920 — July 3, 1981)

Martin played Artemus Gordon on the TV series *The Wild Wild West*.

Ross Martin (left) with Robert Conrad in *The Wild Wild West*

Werner Klemperer (March 22, 1920 — December 6, 2000)

Klemperer is best known as Colonel Klink from the sitcom *Hogan's Heroes*.

James E. Brown (March 22, 1920 — April 11, 1992)

Actor James E. Brown is best known for playing Rip Masters in the TV series *The Adventures of Rin Tin Tin*.

Virginia Grey (March 22, 1917 — July 31, 2004)

Grey debuted in the 1927 silent film version of *Uncle Tom's Cabin* as Little Eva, and went on to a long movie and TV career. She famously had a long relationship with Clark Gable.

Lew Wasserman (March 22, 1913 — June 3, 2002)

Talent agent Lew Wasserman is credited both with assembling and later dismantling the studio system, and also managed the comedy team of Dean Martin and Jerry Lewis.

Karl Malden (March 22, 1912 — July 1, 2009)

Malden (right) won an Academy Award for his role in *A Streetcar Named Desire* and played General Omar Bradley in *Patton*. He starred in the 1970s TV series *The Streets of San Francisco* and was a spokesman for American Express in the 1970s and 1980s.

Wilfred Brambell (March 22, 1912 — January 18, 1985)

Brambell was known to British audiences for his role in the TV sitcom *Steptoe and Son*, and is more generally known for playing Paul McCartney's grandfather in the film *A Hard Day's Night*.

Joseph Schildkraut (March 22, 1896 — January 21, 1964)

Actor Joseph Schildkraut made the transition from silent to talking motion pictures, receiving an Academy Award nomination for his role as Alfred Dreyfus in 1937's *The Life of Emile Zola*, but is best known for playing Otto Frank in the 1959 film *The Diary of Anne Frank*.

Chico Marx (March 22, 1887 — October 11, 1961)

Leonard "Chico" Marx was one of the members of the film and comedy troupe the Marx Brothers. His persona was that of an Italian con artist.

The Marx Brothers (top to bottom): Chico, Harpo, Groucho,
and Zeppo

Music and Dance

Beverley Knight (March 22, 1973 —)

British soul singer Knight was made a Member of the British Empire by Queen Elizabeth II for her charitable work as well as for her contributions to music.

Stephanie Mills (March 22, 1937 —)

Mills won a Grammy for her performance of "Never Knew Love Like This Before."

James House (March 22, 1955 —)

Country music artist James House charted with "This is Me Missing You" in 1995.

Andrew Lloyd Webber (March 22, 1948 —)

Composer and theatrical producer Andrew Lloyd Weber won seven Tony Awards, three Grammys, an Academy Award, and both a knighthood and a peerage from Queen Elizabeth II. His famous works include *The Phantom of the Opera, Jesus Christ Superstar*, and *Cats*.

Keith Relf (March 22, 1943 — May 14, 1976)

Relf was the lead singer and harmonica player for The Yardbirds, and was inducted into the Rock and Roll Hall of Fame with the rest of the group.

George Benson (March 22, 1943 —)

Noted jazz guitarist George Benson received a star on the Hollywood Walk of Fame.

Jeremy Clyde (March 22, 1941 —)

Musician and actor Jeremy Clyde is best known as half of the 1960s folk-rock duo Chad & Jeremy, and for his roles in the British TV series *Crossbow* and *Is It Legal?*

Jeremy Clyde (right) with Patty Duke from *The Patty Duke Show*

Angelo Badalamenti (March 22, 1937 —)

Movie and TV soundtrack composer Badalamenti is best known for his work with David Lynch, including *Blue Velvet, Mulholland Drive*, and *Twin Peaks*.

Roger Whittaker (March 22, 1936 —)

Kenyan singer-songwriter Roger Whittaker is best known for his 1970s hits "New World in the Morning" and "The Last Farewell."

Stephen Sondheim (March 22, 1930 —)

Composer and lyricist Stephen Sondheim won an Academy Award, eight Tony Awards, multiple Grammys, and a Pulitzer Prize. His famous works include *A Funny Thing Happened on the Way to the Forum, A Little Night Music,* and *Sweeney Todd*. He wrote the lyrics for *West Side Story* and *Gypsy*, as well as songs for films including 1981's *Reds* and 1990's *Dick Tracy*.

Ruth Page (March 22, 1899 — April 7, 1991)

American ballerina and choreographer Ruth Page was known for incorporating movements from sports and popular dance into her ballets. She founded the Ruth Page Center for the Arts in Chicago.

Politics, Military, and Public Affairs

Wolf Blitzer (March 22, 1948 —)

CNN television journalist and news anchor Wolf Blitzer became well known for covering the first Gulf War in Kuwait, for which he won a CableACE Award.

Ron Carey (March 22, 1936 — December 11, 2008)

Ron Carey was the first Teamsters president elected by direct vote of the membership, but was expelled when investigators concluded his campaign had been involved in an illegal donation kickback scheme. Although a federal jury later cleared him of all wrongdoing, he was banned from the Teamsters for life.

Orrin Hatch (March 22, 1934 —)

Utah Republican Senator Orrin Hatch was at different times the chair or ranking minority member of the Senate Judiciary Committee and the Senate Finance Committee (depending on which party controls the Senate).

Abulhassan Banisadr (ابوالحسن بنیصدر) (March 22, 1933 —)

Banisadr was first President of Iran following the 1979 Iranian Revolution, and was impeached by the Iranian parliament at the behest of the Ayatollah Khomeni and fled into exile in France.

Al Neuharth (March 22, 1924 —)

Neuharth founded *USA Today*, the Freedom Forum, and the Newseum.

James M. Gavin (March 22, 1907 — February 23, 1990)

General James "Jumpin' Jim" Gavin was the youngest U.S. division commander in World War II. He helped transform the 82nd Infantry Division into the 82nd Airborne Division, and was known for participating in combat drops with his troops, including D-Day.

Arthur Vandenberg (March 22, 1884 — April 18, 1951)

Republican senator from Michigan Arthur Vandenberg was initially known as an opponent of the New Deal, but during World War II became a strong advocate for a bipartisan policy of internationalism. He played a significant role in the establishment of the United Nations, the Marshall Plan, and NATO.

James Timberlake (March 22, 1846 — February 21, 1891)

Deputy U.S. marshal Timberlake led the investigation of the James-Younger Gang, leading to the death of Jesse James at the hands of Robert Ford.

Braxton Bragg (March 22, 1817 — September 27, 1876)

Confederate general Braxton Bragg (right) commanded the Army of Mississippi and won the only major Confederate battle in the western theater, the Battle of Chickamauga. He became the military adviser to Confederate President Jefferson Davis and after the war worked as an engineer.

Stephen Andrews (March 22, 1812 — May 21, 1886)

Andrews was an important abolitionist and wrote several books on individualist anarchism. He was the first person to use the term "scientology" in print, although not in reference to the current religious organization of the same name. He also taught and wrote about the new system of shorthand.

David Swinson Maynard (March 22, 1808 — March 13, 1873)

Maynard was one of the primary founders of Seattle, serving as its first doctor, first business leader, second lawyer, and in many other roles. He first proposed that the city be named for his friend and colleague the Duwamish chief Seattle, who had been helpful in accommodating white settlers.

Kaiser Wilhelm I (March 22, 1797 — March 9, 1888)

As King of Prussia, Wilhelm I appointed Otto von Bismarck as his chancellor, and presided over the unification of Germany, becoming German Emperor (Deutscher Kaiser) in 1871 and ruling until his death.

Detail from a painting of Wilhelm I receiving a letter from Napoleon on the battlefield of Sedan, by Carl Steffeck, 1884

Charles Carroll (March 22, 1723 — March 23, 1783)

Maryland political figure Charles Carroll was a delegate to the Continental Congress and built the colonial mansion Mount Clare, which is now a museum.

Thomas de Mowbray, 1st Duke of Norfolk (March 22, 1366 — September 22, 1399)

Mowbray is best known as a character in the beginning of William Shakespeare's *Richard II*. He was banished along with Henry of Bolingbroke (later King Henry IV) to keep the two from fighting a duel.

Religion

Pat Robinson (March 22, 1930 —)

Televangelist Pat Robinson founded the Christian Broadcasting Network and Regent University, and is best known as the host of the Christian news and talk program *The 700 Club*. He was an unsuccessful candidate for the 1988 Republican presidential nomination.

Sister Lúcia of Fátima (March 22, 1907 — February 13, 2005)

Portuguese nun Sister Lúcia is best known for her visions of the Virgin Mary, for the Three Secrets of Fátima, and for the Miracle of the Sun, witnessed by at least 30,000 people. She was beatified in 2008.

Aryeh Levin (March 22, 1885 — March 28, 1969)

Orthodox rabbi Reb Aryeh was known as the "Father of Prisoners" and the "Tzadik (saint) of Jerusalem" for his work with political prisoners, the poor, and the sick during the British Mandate in Palestine.

Science and Technology

Burton Richter (March 22, 1931 —)

Burton Richter won the Nobel Prize in Physics for leading a team that co-discovered the J/ψ (J/Psi) meson, leading to the "November Revolution" in high-energy physics.

Robert Millikan (March 22, 1868 — December 19, 1953)

American experimental physicist Robert Millikan won the 1923 Nobel Prize in Physics for his work with electron charge and the photoelectric effect.

Sports and Games

Ike Davis (March 22, 1987 —)

First baseman Davis set Mets rookie records for total bases, tied records for bases on balls and extra-base hits, and tied for second-most home runs by a Mets rookie.

Marcus Camby (March 22, 1974 —)

Camby was named NBA Defensive Player of the Year in 2007 and led the league in blocked shots per game.

Elvis Stojko (March 22, 1972 —)

Figure skater Elvis Stojko was a three-time world champion and two-time Olympic silver medalist.

Bob Costas (March 22, 1952 —)

Sportscaster Bob Costas has been prime-time host of a record-setting nine Olympic games.

Jocky Wilson (March 22, 1950 — March 24, 2012)

Wilson won the World Professional Darts Championship in 1982 and 1989.

Don Chaney (March 22, 1946 —)

Chaney is best known as a player and coach for the Boston Celtics. He was NBA Coach of the Year in 1991.

Dave Keon (March 22, 1940 —)

Toronto Maple Leafs centre Dave Keon was inducted into the Hockey Hall of Fame in 1986.

Armin Hary (March 22, 1937 —)

In 1960, Armin Hary won two gold medals in the 1960 Olympics, becoming the first non-American since 1928 to win the Olympic 100 metre race.

Larry Evans (March 22, 1932 — November 15, 2010)

Grandmaster Larry Evans won the U.S. Chess Championship five times and the U.S. Open Chess Championship four times, and wrote or co-wrote over 20 books on chess.

Ed Macauley (March 22, 1928 — November 8, 2011)

NBA player "Easy Ed" Macauley scored 11,234 points in ten NBA seasons, and became the youngest player admitted to the Basketball Hall of Fame.

Jack Crawford (March 22, 1908 — September 10, 1991)

Australian tennis star Jack Crawford was #1 in the world in 1933, and is in the International Tennis Hall of Fame.

Ernie Quigley (March 22, 1880 — December 10, 1960)

Basketball referee, baseball umpire, and football official Ernie Quigley was inducted into the Basketball Hall of Fame in 1961.

Jack Boyle (March 22, 1866 — January 7, 1913)

"Honest Jack" Boyle was a catcher and first baseman for major league baseball teams in Cincinnati, St. Louis, Chicago, New York, and Philadelphia. After his baseball career he opened a saloon. His brother Eddie Boyle was also a major league baseball player.

Jack Boyle

Who Died on March 21?

Arts and Literature

Thomas Hughes (October 20, 1822 — March 22, 1896)

Hughes is best known for his 1857 novel *Tom Brown's School Days*.

Johann Wolfgang von Goethe (August 28, 1749 — March 22, 1832)

Goethe is generally regarded as one of the leading lights of German literature and philosophy. He was a poet, a playwright, a memoirist, a critic, a scientist, and a politician. His best known work is *Faust*.

Film and Theater

William Hanna (July 14, 1910 — March 22, 2001)

William Hanna is best known as Joseph Barbera's partner in the animation studio Hanna-Barbera, which produced such programs as *The Flintstones*, *the Jetsons*, *Scooby-Doo*, and *The Smurfs*.

Walter Lantz (April 27, 1889 — March 22, 1994)

Cartoon director Lantz is best known as the creator of Woody Woodpecker.

Walter Lantz with Woody Woodpecker painting (photo: Alan Light)

Charles Starrett (March 28, 1903 — March 22, 1986)

Starrett played the Durango Kid in the eponymous Columbia Pictures western series.

Mike Todd (June 22, 1909 — March 22, 1958)

Producer Mike Todd is best known for his Academy Award-winning film *Around the World in 80 Days*, and as Elizabeth Taylor's third husband.

Music

Cachao López (September 14, 1918 — March 22, 2008)

Cachao López is considered the inventor of the mambo. He won several Grammy Awards and has a star on the Hollywood Walk of Fame.

Dan Hartman (December 8, 1950 — March 22, 1994)

Singer/songwriter Hartman's hits include "Free Ride," "Instant Reply," and "Love Sensation."

Dave Guard (October 19, 1934 — March 22, 1991)

Guard helped found the Kingston Trio.

Mark Dinning (August 17, 1933 — March 22, 1986)

Pop music star Mark Dinning's biggest hit was 1959's "Teen Angel."

Uncle Dave Macon (October 7, 1870 — March 22, 1952)

Known as the "Dixie Dewdrop," banjo player Uncle Dave Macon was the first star of the Grand Ole Opry.

Richard Leveridge (July 19, 1670 — March 22, 1758)

Singer and composer Richard Leveridge is best known today for the patriotic ballad, "The Roast Beef of Old England," which is used both by the Royal Navy and by the U.S. Marine Corps for formal mess dinners.

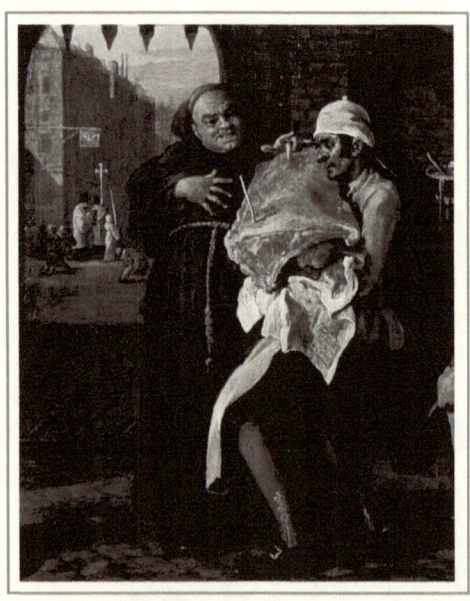

The Roast Beef of Old England by William Hogarth

Politics and Military

Stephen Decatur (January 5, 1779 — March 22, 1820)

Naval officer Stephen Decatur was the first major post-Revolutionary War national hero, serving with distinction in the War of 1812 and the Barbary Wars. He is remembered for an after-dinner toast, "Our Country! In her intercourse with foreign nations may she always be in the right; but right or wrong, our country!" This was later turned into "My country, right or wrong; if right, to be kept right; and if wrong, to be set right," by Carl Schurz.

Decatur Boarding the Tripolitan Gunboat by Dennis Malone Carter

Religion

Jonathan Edwards (October 5, 1703 — March 22, 1758)

Theologian and preacher Jonathan Edwards is known for his classic sermon "Sinners in the Hands of an Angry God." He was the grandfather of Aaron Burr, third Vice President of the United States.

Science and Technology

James Black (June 14, 1924 — March 22, 2010)

Black won the Nobel Prize in Medicine for developing propranolol, used in the treatment of heart disease, and cimetidine, used to treat stomach ulcers. He was knighted for his contributions to medical research.

Gerald Bull (March 9, 1928 — March 22, 1990)

Bull designed the Project Babylon "supergun" for the Iraqi government. He was assassinated in 1990 and the supergun project was stopped.

John Canton (July 31, 1718 — March 22, 1772)

English physicist John Canton developed a method of making artificial magnets, verified Benjamin Franklin's hypothesis that lightning and electricity were the same thing, refuted the generally accepted idea that water was incompressible, and developed the phosphorescent material known as Canton's phosphorous.

Sports

Jumbo Elliott (August 8, 1915 — March 22, 1981)

American track and field coach James "Jumbo" Elliott produced five Olympic gold medal winners between 1956 and 1968, and was inducted into the Track and Field Hall of Fame in 1981.

Peter Revson (February 27, 1939 — March 22, 1974)

Formula One racer Peter Revson won the 1971 Indianapolis 500. He was the nephew of Revlon Cosmetics founder Charles Revson.

The month of March, from the illuminated manuscript *Les Très Riches Heures du duc de Berry*

March: The Third Month

"Up from the sea, the wild north wind is blowing
Under the sky's gray arch;
Smiling I watch the shaken elm boughs, knowing
It is the wind of March."

— *"March," John Greenleaf Whittier*

In ancient Rome, March was the first month of the year. As the first month of spring, in the Mediterranean climate it marked the beginning of the military campaign season. That's why March (Martius) is named in honor of Mars, the Roman god of war.

Although the first month of the year was moved back to January sometime during the transition of Rome from a kingdom to a republic (historians differ), March was the first month of the year in Russia until the end of the 15th Century, and is the first month of the year in many other cultures and religions.

In the northern hemisphere, March 1 marks the beginning of meteorological spring. In the southern hemisphere, March is the equivalent of September, making southern hemisphere March the beginning of autumn.

March is one of the seven months that have 31 days in it. March starts on the same day of the week as November every year, and except for leap years starts on the same day as February. March starts on the same day of the week as the previous June except for leap years, and in leap years starts on the same day as the previous September and December.

March in Other Cultures

In Finland, March is called *maaliskuu* (earthy month). In Ukraine, it's *березень* (birch tree). Other names for March include *Lentmonat* (Saxon), *Hyld-monath* (Angles), and *sušec* (Slovene).

March Symbols

Birthstones: Aquamarine (left) and bloodstone, both representing courage.

Birth Flowers: Daffodils

Daffodils in Bagatelle Park, Paris, France

March Events

Honorary months: Presidents, Congresses, and nations around the world issue proclamations recognizing particular months to honor certain causes. These events generally fall in March. (All US unless otherwise noted.)

- National Nutrition Month
- American Red Cross Month
- Women's History Month (U.S.)

- Irish-American Heritage Month
- Colorectal Cancer Awareness Month
- Fire Prevention Month (The Philippines)

"March Madness": (United States) The NCAA Men's Division I Basketball Championship, popularly known as "March Madness" or the "Big Dance," is a single-elimination tournament to establish the champion college basketball team.

Earth Hour: (International) On Earth Hour, held on the last Saturday of March each year, households and business are urged to turn off all non-essential lights for one hour between 8:30pm to 9:30pm on each person's local time. The goal is to raise awareness of the need to take action on climate change.

Easter Events

The Christian holiday of Easter in Western Christianity is held on the first Sunday after the Paschal Full Moon following the March equinox, which is officially set at March 21 by church reckoning. Easter itself can therefore occur as early as March 22 and as late as April 25, but occurs most often in April.

In Eastern Christianity, which uses the Julian calendar, Easter occurs between April 4 and May 8. This also sets the date for the various events that lead up to Easter, most importantly the events of Holy Week.

La crucifixión by El Greco

Passion Sunday

The fifth Sunday of the Christian season of Lent is known as Passion Sunday in various Protestant denominations and by some traditionalist Catholics. Sometimes, the sixth Sunday of Lent is referred to as Passion Sunday, but it is more commonly known as Palm Sunday. Passion Sunday starts the two-week Passiontide, which ends on Holy Saturday, the day before Easter, commemorating the day that Jesus's body was laid in the tomb. The fifth Sunday of Lent can occur as early as March 8 (though the next time it will be that early is in 2285 CE), and as late as April 11.

Palm Sunday

The moveable feast of Palm Sunday commemorates the triumphant entry of Jesus into Jerusalem, an event mentioned in all four gospels. In many Christian churches, palm leaves are distributed to the worshippers. The earliest date for Palm Sunday is March 15, and the latest is April 18.

Maundy Thursday

The Thursday before Easter is Maundy Thursday, when the Last Supper took place. The earliest day it can occur is March 19, and the latest it can occur is April 22.

Good Friday

Good Friday, observed during Holy Week on the Friday preceding Easter Sunday, commemorates the crucifixion of Jesus and his death at Calvary. Because of its relation to Easter, the earliest day it can occur is March 20, and the latest it can occur is April 23.

Holy Saturday

Sometimes called Easter Eve or Black Saturday, Holy Saturday commemorates the day in which Jesus's body lay in the tomb. Some mistakenly refer to this day as "Easter Saturday," but that properly describes the Saturday following Easter, the last day of Easter Week. The earliest it can occur is March 21, and the latest it can occur is April 24.

Easter

Easter celebrates the resurrection of Jesus Christ on the third day after his crucifixion. In the liturgical calendar, Easter follows the season of Lent, and begins the period known as Eastertide, which ends on Pentecost Sunday. Easter is observed religiously in a morning service.

In the U.S., it's also common to decorate Easter eggs and make Easter baskets of eggs and candy, often with the Easter bunny as a symbol.

The White House traditionally hosts an egg hunt, and many communities have Easter parades.

Easter customs around the world include bonfires (Cyprus, western Sweden), men spanking women with a ceremonial whip (Czech Republic and Slovakia), egg fighting (Bulgaria), cross-country skiing and reading murder mysteries (Norway), and children dressed as witches collecting candy door-to-door (other Nordic countries).

Easter Eggs

March Zodiac Signs

From the perspective of someone on Earth, the Sun appears to move through the sky throughout the year, along a path astronomers call the ecliptic plane. The ecliptic plane is divided into twelve constellations, known as the zodiac, based on traditionally observed patterns of stars. On your birthday, you can't see your constellation, because it's part of the daytime sky.

The zodiac was first developed by Babylonian astronomers about 2,500 years ago. Because they were unaware that the Earth wobbles like a spinning top (a motion known as *precession*), they didn't make allowance for the fact that the Sun's path through the zodiac changes over time.

That means there are now two sets of dates for your birth sign. The *tropical* dates are the original Babylonian dates; the *siderial* dates tell you where the Sun actually appears as it moves along its annual path.

In siderial reckoning, March 21 is in Pisces, but in tropical astrology, March 21 is the first day of Aries. (In some calculations, the transition between Pisces and Aries is related to the first day of the March equinox, meaning that March 20 in some years is the first day of tropical Aries.)

Pisces

Tropical February 20 to March 20

Siderial March 15 to April 14

In the Roman legend of Venus and her son Cupid, they escaped the clutches of Typhon, known as the "father of all monsters," by transforming into fish and tying themselves together with rope. That's why the name Pisces is plural for fish. The constellation appears as a somewhat ragged "V" shape, representing the rope, with the "fish" located at the two rope ends.

In astrology, Pisces is a water sign, compatible with the other water signs Cancer and Scorpio, as well as with the earth signs Taurus, Virgo, and Capricorn. Pisceans are supposed to be imaginative, compassionate, unworldly, secretive, and escapist.

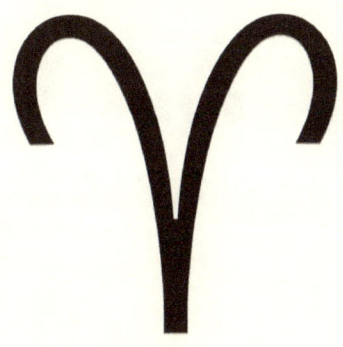

Aries

Tropical March 21 to April 19

Siderial April 15 to May 15

In Greek mythology, Aries is a ram with golden wings and golden wool who rescued the twins Phrixus and Helle from certain death. Although Helle died in the rescue attempt, the grateful Phrixus sacrificed the ram to Zeus. The golden fleece from the sacrificed ram played a prominent part in the later myth of Jason and the Argonauts.

In astrology, Aries, a fire sign, is compatible with the other fire signs of Gemini, Leo, and Sagittarius, and to a lesser extent with air signs Scorpio and Libra. Arians are supposed to adventurous, enthusiastic, quick-tempered, and impulsive.

What Day of the Week is March 21?

On what day of the week does March 21 fall?

Surprisingly, this isn't an easy question. Because the calendar year is 365 days long (366 in leap years), it doesn't divide evenly by the seven days of the week.

Also, the Earth goes around the Sun in about 365-1/4 days, so a calendar tends to drift over time. That's why the same date falls on different weekdays in different years.

This is made even more complicated by a change in calendars that took place in 1582. Our modern calendar has its roots in ancient Rome, in a calendar reform conducted by Julius Caesar. Caesar commissioned mathematicians to attack the problem, and came up with the idea of *leap years,* and thus standardized the calendar for centuries to come. This was called the *Julian calendar.*

Over time, however, the small errors in Caesar's calculation compounded. That's why Pope Gregory XIII commissioned the *Gregorian calendar,* used in most of the world today. Some countries converted in 1582, when the calendar was first developed; some converted later; other still haven't changed.

Gregorian and Julian aren't the only types of calendars. The Hebrew year, the Islamic year, and many other calendars are used in different parts of the world and among different people.

You can convert Gregorian dates to other calendars, including the Hebrew calendar, the Islamic calendar, and even the Mayan calendar by visiting the Fourmilab Calendar Converter at http://www.fourmilab.ch/documents/calendar/.

A 50-year brass perpetual calendar.

Copyright, Credit, and Contact

Follow Us

Our blog Dobson's Improbable History features short articles on events and people associated with each day, and updates several times each week. Get the latest on Twitter @SidewiseThinker.

Contact Us

Find an error or a format problem? Want information about the series, about us, or about when the volume for your special day might be available? Please email us at editor@timespinnerpress.com.

Sources and Art Credits

All art and photographs are either in the public domain or used under a Creative Commons license. Attribution is provided where requested by the copyright owner or when of historical significance, listed below. Most images are from Wikimedia Commons.

- The cover photograph of lasers being used by the Naval Surface Warfare Center is a U.S. Navy photo taken by Greg Vojtko, and is in the public domain as a work of the U.S. federal government.

- The photograph of a 1963 laser in the National Museum of American History was taken by Daderot and was released by the copyright holder into the public domain.

- The illustration of Massasoit and governor John Carver smoking a peace pipe is in the public domain because its copyright has expired. The original is in the collection of the Sutro Library in San Francisco.

- The Stamp Act stamp is in the public domain because it was created by the government of the U.K. prior to 1963.

- The 2011 photograph of the Emerald Buddha was taken by Gremel Madolora, and is used here under the Creative Commons Attribution-Share Alike 3.0 Unported license.

- The photograph of the Flying Wallendas was taken by Porterlu of the Wikipedia Project, who released it into the public domain.

- The photograph of Comet Hale-Bopp was taken in 1997 by Philipp Salzgeber, and is used here under the Creative Commons Attribution-Share Alike 2.0 Austria license. It is a featured picture on Wikimedia Commons. http://salzgeber.at/astro/pics/9703293.html.

- The 1887 illustration by Randolph Caldecott from The Diverting History of John Gilpin is a featured picture on

Wikimedia Commons, and is in the collection of the Library of Congress. It is in the public domain because its copyright has expired.

- The photograph *Scherzo di Follia*, featuring La Castiglione, in in the collection of the Musée d'Orsay, and is in the public domain because its copyright has expired. It is taken here from the Google Art Project.

- The photograph of the Statue of Freedom by Thomas Crawford was taken by the office of the Architect of the Capitol, and is in the public domain as a work of the U.S. federal government.

- The self-portrait of Anton Raphael Mengs is from a private collection, and is a copy (by the artist) of his portrait in the Quadreria dell'Accademia Ligustica di Belle Arti in Genoa, Italy. The image is in the public domain because its copyright has expired.

- The self-portrait of Anthony van Dyck is from a private collection. The image is in the public domain because its copyright has expired.

- The photograph of Reese Witherspoon in the Oval Office is an official White House photo by Pete Souza, and is in the public domain as a work of the U.S. federal government.

- The publicity photograph of Leonard Nimoy and William Shatner from *Star Trek* is in the public domain because it was published in the U.S. between 1923 and 1977 without a copyright notice.

- The publicity photograph from *The Wild Wild West* is in

the public domain because it was published in the U.S. between 1923 and 1977 without a copyright notice.

- The 1953 trailer screenshot of Karl Malden from *I Confess* is in the public domain because it was published in the U.S. between 1923 and 1977 without a copyright notice.

- The 1931 publicity photograph of the Marx Brothers by Ralph F. Stitt is in the Library of Congress Prints and Photographs Division. It is in the public domain because its copyright was not renewed.

- The publicity photograph of Jeremy Clyde with Patty Duke from *The Patty Duke Show* is in the public domain because it was published in the U.S. between 1923 and 1977 without a copyright notice.

- The photograph of Braxton Bragg is in the collection of the Library of Congress Prints and Photographs Division. It is in the public domain because its copyright has expired.

- The detail from the painting *General Reille überbringt König Wilhelm I. auf dem Schlachtfelde von Sedan das Schreiben Kaiser Napoleons* (General Reille brings a letter from the Emperor Napoleon to King Wilhelm I on the battlefield of Sedan) by Carl Steffeck is in the public domain because its copyright has expired.

- The Old Judge Cigarettes baseball card of Jack Boyle is from Benjamin K. Edwards Baseball Card Collection in the Library of Congress Prints and Photographs Division. It is in the public domain because its copyright has expired.

- The painting *La crucifixión* by El Greco is located in the Museo del Prado. It is in the public domain because its copyright has expired.

- The photograph of Czechoslovakian Easter eggs was taken by Jan Kameníček, who has released the image into the public domain.

- The 50-year perpetual calendar photograph is in the public domain.

Timespinner Press